Rockies Autumn Haiku

poems & photographs

Judith Lauter

to Ken

my mountain man

Photo credits

Cover and interior photographs by the author (single exception is the last image, public-domain National Park Service photo by R. Robinson, 1952); back cover photo from the author's collection.

This book was printed in the United States of America.

Rev. date: 03/06/2014

To order additional copies of this book, contact:
Xlibris LLC
1-888-795-4274
www.Xlibris.com
Orders@Xlibris.com

Contents

Preface

Growing up in Austin TX taught me the dramatic differences between flat land (the Texas central prairies to our east, where my family rarely ventured) and lands of glorious ups and downs (the Texas hill country in and to the west of Austin).

Thus, even though I spent my later childhood and adolescence in lush, green central Michigan, the dry, rocky Texas hills stayed in my mind. When in 1965, still in Michigan, I met the person who would become my "mountain man," we chose Tucson AZ – with mountains in all directions – as our best choice for his first teaching job and our first home. The inaugural book in my photo-haiku series, *Sonora Spring Haiku* (2013), reflects some of the wonders we saw in Arizona.

After Tucson we moved to Denver briefly, and fell in love with the Colorado Rockies. Although grad school and jobs conspired to send us elsewhere – to St. Louis, Oklahoma, and most recently to East Texas (*Year of Haiku*, 2013; and *Pineywoods Summer Haiku* and *Lanana Creek Haiku*, both 2014) – our hearts have remained in the mountain west.

So for the past several years we have spent a month or so every late summer in the Rockies of northern New Mexico and southern Colorado. The photos and poems in this book represent our experiences there: in the Sangre de Cristos outside Santa Fe NM; the Moreno Valley's high cool park near Wheeler Peak east of Taos; and the gorgeous country around Gunnison and Crested Butte CO.

Fall is our favorite season in the mountains. The Rockies are staggering year-round, but in autumn, they are in their full glory. Through all the transformations – from the delicious greens of "high-cool high summer," to the time when entire mountainsides of aspens turn gold, and then the gradual leaning toward winter – the peaks, valleys, and high parks of the Rockies are incomparable. This book is a small tribute to that grand beauty.

— JLL, Angel Fire NM, September 2013

Rockies Autumn Haiku

Last Weeks of High Summer

Aspen in the Carson National Forest near Angel Fire NM

August Arrival

High summer in high places,
the best place to be:
cool air, aspens like water.

Mountain Afternoons

1.
To swing in a hammock, with
aspen all around,
in a sphere of aspen sound.

2.
Breeze zithers aspen; dozing,
I rock in my bowed
hammock, humming too with joy.

3.
Wind makes an aeolian
harp of my hammock
strings, and so sings me to sleep.

Follow the Emerald-Brick Road

Aspen palaces, spirals
of spruce — chlorophyll's
magic behind the green door.

Embodiment

Lets me come close to greet her:
gaze of black aspen
eyes, blonde coat silken as grass.

Clicking Grasshopper Haiku

One lights on my shoulder, then
takes off again, both
of us counting syllables.

Continental Thermals

Airflows shared by crows, vultures,
hawks, pumped up here from
a thousand miles of prairie.

Intimations of Fall

Southern end of the Moreno Valley near Angel Fire NM

The End of Summer

Cold rain today, then early
next morning mist fills
the valleys deeper than snow.

Footsteps after Rain

See where the feet go: twin leaf–
prints side by side, two–
toed walk, slipping on slick spots.

Making Plans

Cottontail contemplates rocks
to hide in when all
blooms hide in warrens of snow.

Study in Whites

Climbing white cloud warns white trees
another white is
on its way: colder, ice-blue.

Late Butterfly

Butterfly sees her shadow,
steps carefully from
summer toward autumn's cold sand.

The Golden Days

Looking north up the Ohio Creek valley near Gunnison CO

First Gold

Willows and cottonwoods turn
first, xanthophyll and
carotene light up the creeks.

Mountain Parade

All along the ridges, lines
of aspen dance to
wind's drum, yellow hair flying.

Along state highway 114, north of Saguache CO

Cosmic Gold

Supercharged with heav'nly fire,
trees are solar flares,
novas around every bend.

Light Show

Sunlight and shorter days set
trees ablaze: off steep
green slopes, firefalls of aspen.

Invitational

Be baptized in yellow air,
sunlight stored through long
summer days — this radiance.

Volcano Memento

Old lava talus burns new
as matchstick trees let
red-gold leaves like sparks fly up.

Leaning Toward Winter

In the Sangre de Cristos near Santa Fe NM

Transitions

Most gone to snow-white bones, but
here and there a crowd
won't give up the gold parade.

Aspen Abacus

Light breeze fingers golden coins,
lets them fall, counting
leaf by leaf the days till snow.

Patience

Aspen bones white against white,
tips in sprays, wrapped tight,
looking past snowfalls toward May.

Continental Divide seen from the west, above Taylor Reservoir south of Crested Butte CO

When the Peaks Turn White

Our soft bare skin was not made
for these climes — so when
you hear snow's muffled footfall,

leave high places to sleepers,
burrowers, those who
can grow their own shaggy coats.

Epilogue

Elk in light snow (National Park Service photo, R. Robinson, 1952)

Legacy

My oldest girl, when she was just a baby,
I could tell she would be a grandmother —
she was strong and had good sense.
When I laid her down under manzanita
to sleep while I grazed, she stayed
as if she knew what it was for, and lay
so still. Other calves don't have that much sense.
Their moms, either — they neglect to lick a calf

completely dry, or forget to eat
the droppings, or they stray too far
and sometimes don't get back ahead of the wolves.
Those calves don't last too long, those
women either, for that matter.
The wolves are always there.
They change from time to time
but this woman's pack has been here

for years, she's a grandmother
too. Her group is good about taking
mostly only the ones who won't last.
I lost a baby to them once,
the one I carried that hard winter when
there wasn't enough to eat, he
was sickly from the first.
My oldest girl has had her scrapes and cuts

but she always healed quickly,
another good sign. There are two more
grandmother-types like her now — one older,
my aunt's girl, and one younger, my youngest

sister's first. We are lucky to have three
already, a comfort to know they're there
so when I get too old or whatever else happens
I can lie down knowing someone capable we watched

grow up is here to take my place.
This valley has been good for us as long as
I can remember — my mother's mother lived here,
all my aunts, their grandmothers too.
The woman who joined us several years ago
came from a valley two ridges to the West.
She knew my oldest sister who went there when
I was just a calf myself. If these wolves change

somehow, start breeding more,
we might change valleys, go two ridges West
and try to share with them, but that would
be hard — better to stay with what we know,
the water we know, the growing things
that always green up just in time for us,
every spring. We come upslope splashing in snowmelt,
our bellies big with babies, and drop them

in the young green grass all together
over three or four cool summer mornings. We lick them dry
and jam our noses down into the tasty shoots
so we can make the milk our babies drink so they
grow up strong and eat the grass themselves.
I remember my oldest girl pulled hard at my teats,
another sign of health. Now the tiny hairs behind
her ears are turning blonde, she is growing up.

The aspen leaves are turning blonde, too,
around the edges. There has been frost the last
few days, it's almost time to go downslope.
Timing the going is everything, of course, just like
coming back. If we leave here too early, the fall rains down
there will not have come, the grass will be too dry.
If we start too late, we can get caught in a wet snow
too deep for our young ones, and we lose some.

That happened when the grandmother before me
died — we found her curled up under the early snow
not moving. Maybe because she was old, she waited
too long. The rest of us barely made it out that time—
I kicked through snow behind my mom, jumping
to keep up. But we all went slow, and we all got out.
The sun on our backs down there felt so warm!
Soon it will be time to go this year.

We can sleep in frost, but I don't like to wait till
snow. My oldest girl sleeps against me these cold nights,
I feel her heartbeat matching mine,
her heat joining mine, making us both warmer.
She and the older one like her will walk up front
with me for the first time on this trip down,
and that's another good thing — they need to learn
the way we always go.

Printed in the United States
By Bookmasters